PORTRAIT
BEFORE DARK

SAINT JULIAN PRESS

POETRY

Praise for PORTRAIT BEFORE DARK

Poems in translation are like visas stamped in our passports to other countries. In *Portrait Before Dark* we are lucky to have Liana Sakelliou's fine poems translated by Aliki Barnstone, the distinguished American poet at ease in Greek, lifting the barrier to a kindred world.

—John Balaban
Empires; Path, Crooked Path

Reading Aliki Barnstone's luminous translation of Liana Sakelliou's wondrously surreal series, *Portrait Before Dark,* is to enter an imaginary garden with real people in it—a bewitching world that is part history and part mystery. The series is based loosely on the life of 20th c. art patron and poet, Edward James, but none of the magic and majesty of these poems is dispelled by any of the facts of James' life. Sakelliou is one of the most prominent poets now writing in Greece, and her marvelous lyricism has found in Barnstone a poet-translator of equal poetic gifts. To read this collection is (as one poem has it) *to mount the stairs of poetry into myth.*

—Cynthia Hogue
In June the Labyrinth

Just what is Portrait Before Dark? Dream, fantasia, magic, tapestry, embroidered ghosts entering a garden, or a forest of dangers. A poetry of myth. You are invited to the undersea palace, to a half-hidden love story. The adventure may be disastrous. Step this way.

—Alicia Ostriker
The Volcano and After: Selected and New Poems 2002-2019

"Desire / fashions delusions," writes Greek poet Liana Sakelliou in this fragmentary sequence of interior correspondences between poet Edward James and ballerina Tilly Losch. Set on James' British estate, these brief bursts of restrained emotion recall the poems of Emily Dickinson and H.D. and the surreal paintings of Leonora Carrington: "Small ghosts enter the garden / and lay themselves out like fabric / for the embroidery needle." Rendered in crisp and resonant English by poet Aliki Barnstone, each poem, "touched by the thread / of a new story," adds to the tapestry of a tumultuous relationship. *Portrait Before Dark* is like a hedge maze in which losing oneself leads to edgy pleasures.

—Michael Waters
Celestial Joyride, Gospel Night

PORTRAIT BEFORE DARK

Liana Sakelliou

translated by
Aliki Barnstone

SAINT JULIAN PRESS
HOUSTON

Published by
SAINT JULIAN PRESS, Inc.
2053 Cortlandt, Suite 200
Houston, Texas 77008

www.saintjulianpress.com

ISBN-13: 978-1-955194-03-7
Library of Congress Control Number: 2022930136

Cover Art: *Within a Dark Forest* by Aliki Barnstone

To our children, Stefanos Schultz and Zoë Barnstone.

—L.S. and A.B.

CONTENTS

PREFACE

LIANA SAKELLIOU

This poem cycle constitutes an imaginary dialogue between the poet and patron of the arts, Edward James, and the Viennese ballerina and star of the 1920's, Tilly Losch.

I began writing these poems in August 2009, when I was serving as writer-in-residence at West Dean College in West Sussex, England. Three days before I was to leave for the U.K., a wildfire surrounded my home and neighborhood. In minutes the pine forest and hillside olive groves were lost. For days, my suitcase and the clothes I'd packed smelled of smoke.

Edward James, the Anglo-American millionaire, gave his estate to a charitable trust, the Edward James Foundation, which includes the mansion, West Dean House, where the college is located. I sat on the satin Mae West Lips Sofa, one of Salvadore Dalí's surrealist sculptures and read James's poems. Through the biographical films that were screened at West Dean, I discovered James's friendships with artists such as Leonora Carrington, Dalí, and René Magritte, and with writers such as Christopher Isherwood, Edith Sitwell, and Evelyn Waugh. He seemed to know everyone of his age. He spoke to Freud, knew members of the Bloomsbury group, and was one of the most generous English patrons of the arts in the early 20th Century. He helped Max Ernst and Dylan Thomas, as well as the aforementioned Carrington, Dalí, and Magritte. In 1933, during his marriage to Losch, James funded Balanchine's first ballet company, Les Ballets 1933, which was the foundation for his American Ballet Company. He commissioned *The Seven Deadly Sins*, a collaboration by Kurt Weil and Bertolt Brecht, featuring Losch as prima ballerina and Lotte Lenya as vocal soloist. Their marriage from 1930-1934 was short and disastrous, and their divorce was a scandal in London society. In 1937, Magritte painted two faceless portraits of

James: "The Pleasure Principle: Portrait of Edward James" and "Not to be Reproduced," to which I refer in my poems.

The setting of West Dean seemed made for children—with topiary birds and spirals, lush flowers, conservatories, and sheep one could pet. I saw portraits of the James family, as well as Cecil Beaton and Man Ray's photos of Edward and Tilly walking through the palace corridors. I liked their faces, their poses. I wanted to write quiet, allusive poems that speak through their voices. The English woodlands serve as a flexible space in which the spaciousness of love merges with the conflicting emotions that the poems call into question.

ALIKI BARNSTONE

Much like Emily Dickinson and H.D., whose work she translates magnificently, Liana Sakelliou is a poet of the ineffable, who makes her feminist vision palpable in the world of her poetry. *Portrait Before Dark* is and is not the story of Edward James and Tilly Losch's marriage and its dissolution. It's about how the story is told, whose voice soars above the forest, and whose voice resists convention, which for women too often is a form of silencing: "You can tell sundry stories / about the same ways of making a life." It's about being in love and losing oneself in another person. It's about reclaiming the self. It's about the urge to bring children into the world and the choice not to. It's about the journey into the forest and about the Earth. It's about climate change. It takes place at the beginning of the twentieth century and it takes place at the beginning of the twenty-first. It doesn't stay fixed in time. It doesn't "take place." It's in England and not, in Greece and not, everywhere and nowhere. As Edward (perhaps it's Edward) says to Tilly (perhaps it's Tilly): "You mount the stairs into myth." So too do these lines of poetry form the stairs, climb them, and rise protean into a new mythology. It's about the trees. It's not "about" a subject but embodies subjectivity.

Let me go back to the trees. The trees are a major actor in *Portrait Before Dark*. The forest "refuses nothing." The forest will "know / to be tender with me." When asked "What happened to you?" The answer is "a bizarre tree electrified me." The forest and the creatures it shelters have agency beyond human perception, even as human actions destroy them. Sakelliou's apocalyptic vision critiques the brutality of patriarchal wealth. Edward (and it is him in this case) proclaims:

> Something rises like smoke
> and, loosing its smelly musk,
> a red fox crosses the woods.
> Its tail catches fire.
> I'm a good shot.

In this scene of smoke and fire, the wounded red fox is not just pitiable, wrenching our hearts, but is the beautiful, magical, and vulnerable animal sacrificed for sport, for the hunter's bragging rights. Perhaps this fox will be taken to the taxidermist and join the other woodland creatures decorating the halls of the castle. I can't help but feel that Tilly (and it is Tilly in this case) left the marriage to escape becoming a trophy. She half muses, half taunts:

> I was once your wife, rich man.
> What did it mean?
> A titillating show?
> A vortex in your years?

I don't mean to imply that Edward is merely the bad guy here; *Portrait Before Dark* is far too nuanced for that kind of dichotomous thinking. He, too, finds himself playing a role assigned to him by the accident of birth, an accident that conferred upon him wealth, privilege, and the tools and weapons to defend the way of life (and death) of his ancestors.

Liana composed *Portrait Before Dark* in the aftermath of wildfires that consumed her neighborhood in 2009. Every year we have borne witness to worsening drought, record heat, and wildfires. One summer, after visiting and working with Liana, I left the island of Poros via the longer ferry route because the highway to Athens was impassable due to fire. The air was full of smoke and ash floating above the sea that reflected gray rather than blue. Last summer Liana and her family had to evacuate their home north of Athens and I could not return with my family to ours a few kilometers away. The sublime beauty of our motherland is burning away, the wide beaches disappearing beneath the rising sea. Greece, like other small countries, is the fox vulnerable to the actions and inactions of the superpowers. Of course, "our motherland" isn't only Greece, it's everyone's motherland. Here, translated for all of you, wherever you are, is our exquisite, sad, hopeful, shared *Portrait Before Dark*.

PORTRAIT
BEFORE DARK

Midway upon the journey of our life
I found myself within a forest dark,
For the straightforward pathway had been lost.

— Dante Alighieri
Tr. Henry Wadsworth Longfellow

Είμαι το αγόρι στα ναυτικά
και δρασκελίζω μαγικά
τη θάλασσα του δάσους·
φυλλόσχημα μαλλιά,
εξωτικά πουλιά τα κατοικούν.
Ένα πνευστό βαθύφωνο κρατώ
να ξεπερνώ λιγοψυχιές.
Το μεταγωγικό είναι άσπρο.
Το φουγάρο του ψηλό.

I am the boy in a sailor suit.
I amble magically
in the sea forest,
exotic birds
in my leafy hair,
holding a tuba
to stave off feeling scared.
The freighter is white,
its smokestack tall.

Ο χρόνος ήταν το απόσταγμα
σ' ένα χρυσό κύπελο με τ' όνομά μου
από τον βασιλιά.
Πατέρα, η μητέρα είναι κόρη του;
Είμαι ο γιος του;
Άρχισα να συλλέγω περιγράμματα,
χρώματα με οικόσημο το μαύρο.

Time was distilled
in a gold goblet etched with my name
given by the king.
Father, is my mother his daughter?
Am I his son?
I began collecting shapes,
colors on a black coat of arms.

Δεν χρειαζόμουν το μαύρο —
το μονότονο σχέδιο, τη μυστικότητα
δίχως το ανθρώπινο είδος.
Θα 'θελα να το ανασυνθέσω ελεύθερα,
να το εξερευνήσω με τη βελόνα
στον κίνδυνο.

Δεν κάνω τίποτα να διώξω τον φόβο,
τσουκνίδες, σκλήθρες, σαρκοφάγα,
ο τεράστιος μανδύας για τον διάβολο.
Μετακινώ τα δάχτυλα πιο πέρα,
κινώ το δάσος προς εμένα.

Ένα είδος αναζήτησης είναι κι αυτό,
μια περιπέτεια αισθήσεων.
Να το αλλάξω;
Τα στοιχειά να μπουν σε κήπο;
Να ποζάρουν σαν υλικό για κέντημα;

I don't need black—
colorless design, the secret
divided from humanity.
I'd like to rebuild from scratch,
explore with my needle
to the point of danger.

I don't need things to ward off fear—
nettles, splinters, carnivores,
or a vast vestment against the devil.
I wave my fingers toward the beyond,
make the forest come to me.

This, too, is a kind of quest,
a sensual adventure.
Shall I change course?
Shall ghosts enter the garden
and lay themselves out like fabric
for the embroidery needle?

Ακατέργαστη άρνηση πνέει
ανάμεσά μας σαν πειρασμός,
σαν απόκληρα κάστρα.

Η προσμονή του χώρου
ένας αγώνας.
Τίποτα δεν αρνείται το δάσος,

ούτε κι αυτό.

Raw refusal blows between us
like temptation,
like condemned castles.

The anticipation of place
is struggle.
The forest refuses nothing,

not even this.

Η σκηνή απαιτεί νύμφες,
καβαλάρηδες αλύγιστους
με σιδερόπλεκτα γάντια,
το φρένιασμα του κυνηγιού.
Έχεις κεφάλι ελαφιού.
Κρέμομαι στο πράσινο χάος
σαν χνουδωτό έντομο.
Εισβολέας οφθαλμός
για να τα βλέπω όλα.

The scene needs nymphs,
stiff horsemen
wearing chain-mail gauntlets,
and the frenzy of the hunt.
You have a deer's head
and I hang in green chaos
like a downy insect.
My eye intrudes
to see it all.

Υπάρχουν πολλοί τρόποι αφήγησης
για τα ίδια μοντέλα ύπαρξης.
Η φυσική γοητεία του βασιλιά,
της μητέρας, των φίλων τους στις
φωτογραφίες των διαδρόμων.

Βυθίζονται πίσω από συστάδες
δέντρων προσηλωμένων
στη σκοτεινή γη.

Δεν μπορώ να διαχωρίσω το δάσος
από το πέρασμα των ζώων,
τις αιμάτινες φτέρες,
τον γδούπο στις φυλλωσιές.

You can tell sundry stories
about the same ways of making a life—
the natural charm
of the king, the mother,
and their friends in photos
along the corridors' walls.

They sink behind the grove,
committed to the dark earth.

I can't discern the woods
from the animals passing by,
the bloodied ferns,
the thudding in the foliage.

Μαύρες μπότες, καμιζόλες
από βατίστα,
καπέλα με φτερά.
Η μητέρα φορούσε μεταξωτά
στο χρώμα του στρειδιού
και περιδέραια μαργαριταριών
πλέκονταν στον λαιμό της.

Υπέβαλα την απουσία της
σε μεταπλάσεις.
Της είπα,
Αντί για πρόσωπα
ας μιλήσουμε
για το ένα πρόσωπο.

Black boots, cotton batiste camisoles,
feathered hats.
My mother wore silk
the color of oysters
and pearl necklaces
looped around her throat.

I turned her absence
to transfiguration.
I said to her,
Let's not talk about faces.
Let's talk about the face.

Τα μάτια σου με σάρωσαν.
Οι κυματισμοί επεκτάθηκαν
στα φυλλώματα μες στο φαράγγι.

Ψιλόβρεχε.

Τίποτα δεν συγκρίνεται
με το δάσος, είπες—
Υπήρξες κάποτε πέρα απ' τα φύλλα;

Your eyes scanned me.
Ripples spread on foliage
in the gorge.

A light rain.

Nothing compares
with woodlands, you said—
Were you ever there beyond the leaves?

Με άγγιξες κι άρχισα να μεγαλώνω —
απρόβλεπτες ρίζες,
πλούσιο καφετί.

Κάτι σαν ζούγκλα
περιέλουζε τα φύλλα μου
κάνοντας ελιγμούς.

You touched me and I began to grow
rich brown roots,
unforeseen.

Something like a jungle
encircled my leaves,
snakelike.

Πέταλα παντού σκορπά—
μπαίνουνε στα μαλλιά,
τραβούν το φόρεμά μου
μέχρι κι εγώ ν' ανθίσω
όπως εκείνη που αγγίζεται
ποιος ξέρει από τι.

Και με ρωτά ο ιπποκόμος,
Τι σας συνέβη;
Αλλόκοτο δέντρο, απαντώ,
ηλεκτροφόρο.

Petals sprinkle everywhere—
tangle in my hair,
stick on my dress
until I, too, flower
like one touched
by who knows what.

A horse groomer asks,
What happened to you?
I answer, a bizarre tree
electrified me.

Παρασύρεσαι από τον χρόνο
με όλες τις ενδείξεις του.
Αγγίζεσαι από τον μίτο
μιας νέας αφήγησης.
Αναμφίβολα σε συγκινεί.

Time drives you around
with all its omens
and you're touched by the thread
of a new story.
Without a doubt, it moves you.

Θα συγκινήσω τα δέντρα,
θα χορέψω γι' αυτά.
Ειδοποίησέ τα
να γίνουν τρυφερά μαζί μου.

Όταν χορεύω
συναντώ τους ήχους τους
και παρασυρμένη
σπάω τη σιωπή.

Θα χαλαρώσω στα μάτια σου μετά —
ξημέρωμα στο δάσος ή καταβύθιση.

Σαν υπνοβάτης αναρριχώμαι στη σκάλα
που οδηγεί στον ουρανό σου.

I'll move the trees,
dancing for them,
and let them know
to be tender with me.

When I dance
I meet their sound
and, bewitched,
shatter their silence.

Later your eyes will relax me
and I'll wake or sink in the woods.

Like a sleepwalker I climb stairs
that lead to your sky.

Ανεβαίνεις τη σκάλα του μύθου.
Όλα όσα έχω να σου πω
χάνονται.

Βλέπω τη γραμμή των ώμων,
το κεφάλι γερμένο προς τα πίσω,
τα πράσινα μάτια μισόκλειστα.

Επινοείς τον χορό
καθώς ανοίγεις την πόρτα,

απλώνεις το χέρι κι αργόσυρτα μπαίνω
στο δάσος
μαζί σου.

You mount the stairs into myth.
All I have to tell you
is lost.

I watch your torso's form,
head tilted back,
green eyes half-closed.

It's your choreography
when you open the door,

stretch out your hand, and I
enter the woods in slow motion
at your side.

Ένιωσα την ανάγκη
να συνδεθώ με τον αιώνα
της ιστορίας σου —
τις αντίκες του σπιτιού,
τις αναρίθμητες κάμαρες.

Το είδος της σιωπής
που έπεφτε.
Το μέσα σπίτι μονάχο.
Την ανάσα των δέντρων επάνω σου
πριν το σκοτάδι.

Ξαφνικό αίσθημα

σαν έρωτας.

The need struck me
to enter the era
of your entire history—
your mansion's antiques
and countless ballrooms.

A sort of silence
that fell.
Dwelling's solitary interior.
The trees breathed on you
before dark.

I'm suddenly overcome

as if falling in love.

Το βλέμμα σου — πράσινο ή ασημένιο
ανάλογα με το άνοιγμα
του φεγγαριού — πουλί, η ανάσα,
άρρυθμο.

Άνασσα, θα γίνεις δική μου.
Μόλις ησυχάσεις θα σε φάω.
Λαμπρός υμέναιος σαν επέλαση.

Ανοίξτε τη βαριά πόρτα,
το κόκκινο παχύ χαλί να ξεχυθεί,
οι πανοπλίες, οι θυρεοί,
τα τρόπαια με τα ελαφίσια κεφάλια.

Your gaze is green or silver—
according to the moon's opening—
your breath a bird's, quick.

Your Majesty, you'll be mine.
When you calm down, I'll eat you,
our opulent wedding like a battle.

Swing open the heavy door,
unroll the plush red carpet
to suits of armor, coats of arms,
mounted deer heads.

Ετοιμασία ταξιδιού —
νέες σκέψεις
στη χορωδία χνουδωτών φιδιών,
σαράντα σκύλων, εκατό πουλιών.

Κυρίως όμως αποζητούσα
μια πρόκληση συγκίνησης.

Χάραξε τα όρια και κάλεσέ με
σαν εκείνο το μαγεμένο
που μένει κρυμμένο
στο δάσος.

Travel preparations:
new ideas
about a chorus of furred snakes,
forty hounds, one hundred birds.

Even more than all this, I wanted
my senses stirred.

Draw the border and beckon to me
as if I were that bewitched spirit
who keeps hidden
in the woods.

Κρατώ τα χέρια σου στα δικά μου
και φαντάζομαι τις σκοτεινές αλέες
έξω από το γοτθικό παράθυρο —
η κρυφή ζωή ανταποκρίθηκε
στην πέτρα που έριξες στο τζάμι.

Έγινε μεγάλη τελετή όταν γεννήθηκα,
πυροτεχνήματα στον αέρα
κι ο βασιλιάς χαμογελούσε.
Έπειτα μεταμόρφωνα την κούνια
σε παλάτι κάτω από τη θάλασσα.

I hold your hands in mine
and conjure the dark grove
outside my gothic window.
A secret life answered the pebble
you threw at the glass.

They hosted a gala when I was born,
fireworks in the air. The king smiled.
As I grew I transformed my cradle
into a palace below the sea.

Συμβαίνει αυτό τη στιγμή
μιας αναχώρησης,
συμπεριφορά ενστικτώδης,
κάτι με τρόπο τελεσίδικο.

Θα μπορούσε ν' αποδοθεί
στη σιωπή του βυθού.
Ίσως πάντα να γίνεται έτσι.
Κι ωστόσο μοιάζει παράξενο.

It happens the instant of goodbye,
an instinctive act,
some final gesture.

Maybe it flows from
the silence of the deep.
Maybe it always happens this way.
And yet it seems odd.

Μ' όλο το ψύχος
με βγάζεις απ' τον βυθό
στο ξέφωτο.

Θρόισμα, φτιάχνεις ομόκεντρους κύκλους
γύρω σου,
βρύα από βελούδο στον κορμό σου.

Αλλάζεις την πυκνότητα του πέπλου.
Το διαπερνάς αργά
σαν μυστικό.

Μια στάση στον χορό, μια έκσταση.
Χορεύεις πάνω από το δάσος
Ομφάλη, Λήδα, Ιόλη όσο ποτέ.

Even with all the cold
you lift me from the deep
into a glade:

A rushing sound—
and I see ripples form around you,
your torso covered with velvet moss.

Your veil thins—
you're passing through
like a secret.

A pause in your dance—an ecstasy—
then above the forest, you pirouette
more Omphale, Leda, and Ioli than ever.

Φόρεμα όλο πράσινα μάτια
θα παραγγείλω, να το ακούω να θροΐζει, να
σε τυλίγει, μετά να ξεδιπλώνεται σαν τέλος
θεατρικής πράξης.

Φόρεμα σηρικό σαν επιφάνεια λίμνης,
να το φιλήσω απαλά
ενώ η γλώσσα του νερού
θα του γλύφει την ούγια.

I'll order a dress
the tint of your green eyes
to hear the folds swishing around you,
the way the curtain unfolds
at the close of a play's act.

I'll softly kiss
a dress, silk like a lake's surface,
as the water's tongue
licks its hem.

Με ήχο μουσικό
στις άκρες των δακτύλων μου
χορεύω στον σμάλτο της μπανιέρας.

Αφροί κυκλώνουν τις ρώγες,
κολλούν, τυλίγουν,
πνίγουν την πλάτη μου.

I dance to the music
on pointe
on the bathtub's enamel.

Soapsuds encircle my nipples;
sticking, enveloping,
drowning my back.

Κλυδωνίζεσαι στα κύματα
σαν να φοβάσαι μην σε πνίξει
η αδιόρατη δίνη της πορσελάνης.

Θ' αποτυπώσω τα πέλματά σου,
νωπά απ' το μπάνιο,
στο χλόινο χαλί της σκάλας.

Ο πόθος
δημιουργεί παραισθήσεις.

Η σκάλα οδηγεί στην κάμαρά μας.
Το φως θα μας βρει σμαραγδί.

You undulate in the waves
as if you're afraid of drowning
in the unseen porcelain vortex.

I will weave the imprint of your footsteps
wet from the bath
on the stairs' grassy carpet.

Desire
fashions delusions.

The stairs lead to our bedroom.
The light will find us emerald.

Ήμουν ήδη πνιγμένος από παιδί.
Θέλω να βγω στην επιφάνεια,
να σε κοιτάξω
χωρίς ν' ανασαίνω.

I was already drowned as a child.
I want to rise to the surface
and look at you
breathless.

Η σχέση μας θυμίζει
εωθινή διάθλαση φωτός —
τρελαίνει τα έντομα μες το σκοτάδι.
Τα δάχτυλά μου γίνονται πουλιά,
στροβιλίζονται στη μυρωδιά
του νωπού δέρματός μου.
Χορεύω, ξεχνιέμαι, χορεύω.
Χρειάζεσαι κληρονόμο.
Ιδού εγώ, εν γαστρί φέρουσά σοι.

Our love recalls
daybreak's refracting rays—
the insects go crazy without the dark.
My fingers become birds
spinning in the scent
of my fresh skin.
I dance, forgetting myself, I dance.
You need an heir.
Here am I. I carry you in my womb.

Το μόνο θαύμα. Αυθύπαρκτο.
Με κατακλύζει.
Μετακινεί το πέπλο της οδύνης παραπέρα.

Ο ουρανός βαθαίνει.
Κρατώ τις ακτίνες της αγάπης
και προετοιμάζομαι για τη συνάντηση.

Ειδήμονας της εφηβείας μου
θα διανύσω μαζί του τον δρόμο της
δέσμευσης ζαλισμένος, σαν νάχω πιει.

The one miracle, sovereign,
engulfs me,
moves aside pain's veil.

The sky deepens.
I hold love's radiance
and make ready to meet him.

Conscious of my own youth,
I'll walk beside him on devotion's path,
dizzy, as if an inebriate.

Έρχεται από πολύ μακριά.
Δεν το αναγνωρίζω.

Το σκίρτημά του
στοιχειώνει στα σπλάχνα μου.
Είναι πέτρα σε πλοίο, υποταγή.

Και η αντήχησή του στα χείλη
μπλέκεται με τη μοίρα για τελειότητα.

Να ξαναγίνω πλάσμα
της φαντασίας σου
ή αν θες ο σκοτεινός σου καθρέφτης.

Δίχως αυτό.

It comes from far, far away.
I don't acknowledge it.

Its quickening haunts me inside.
It's a boulder on a ship, submission.

Its tone on my lips
conflicts with my fate, a dancer's
perfection.

Let me be the creature
of your fantasy again
or your dark mirror if you want.

Without it.

Δεν βλέπω πια τα δέντρα,
βλέπω τις σκέψεις σου.
Η αλλαγή του καιρού απλώνεται
στο δάσος. Τα πουλιά μετεωρίζονται.
Νυχτώνει.

No longer do I see the trees;
I see your thoughts.
A change of weather spreads over
the forest. Birds glide.
Night falls.

Ευκίνητα τα δάχτυλά μου
σου φανερώνουν την αγωνία
του έσχατου χορού.
Συμπυκνώνομαι σ' αυτά που υπήρξαν.
Μια δοκιμασία ως το τέλος.

Deftly my fingers tell you
the agony of the final dance.
I'm distilled into what was—
a trial to the end.

Μια νύχτα είδα τον πατέρα μου
ανάμεσα σ' εμένα και στη φωτιά.
Δεν είδα τα μάτια του,
μονάχα το σχήμα του σώματός του.
Φορούσε τα ρούχα που αγαπούσε
ενώ η φωτιά έλαμπε μέσα τους.
Σκότωσα κατά λάθος
μια λευκή κουκουβάγια.
Έμεινες έγκυος. Πήρες κινίνο.
Άρχισες να αιμορραγείς.

One night I saw my father
between the flames and me.
I couldn't see his eyes,
only the shape of his body.
He wore the clothes he loved
illuminated by fire.
I killed a white owl by mistake.
You got pregnant. Took quinine.
Began to bleed.

Φορώ γυαλιά ηλίου
με σκελετό κουκουβάγιας,
είσαι τυλιγμένος σ' ένα μπουρνούζι —
ο μήνας του μέλιτος.

Υπάρχει κάτι στο κενό —αχνίζει
ανάλαφρη ζωή, πάνω απ' την άλλη.

Μόνο σε ότι σπάζει φαίνεται το φως.
Αγάπη με τρόπο απόμακρο.

Η θάλασσα μας τραβά προς αυτό —
δεν γνωρίζουμε

τι ξεσκεπάζουμε.

I wear sunglasses with owl frames.
You have a robe wrapped around you—
our honeymoon.

Something in the emptiness—
a light life streams above the other life.

Only in brokenness does the light come
in—love from far away.

The sea draws us to this—
we don't know

what we expose.

Ο κύκλος της δημιουργίας
στροβιλίζεται γύρω από μια λάμψη
μέχρι να εκραγεί κι αυτή
στο τελευταίο μέρος της Ηρωικής.

Ασημικά, πορτρέτα, πολυέλαιοι
στριφογυρίζουν γύρω μας
μα δεν χορεύω πια μαζί σου
στο δίχτυ πάνω από τον θάνατο.

The circle of creation spins
around a radiance
until it too explodes
in the last movement of Eroica.

Silverware, portraits, chandeliers
spin around us
but I don't dance with you anymore
in the net above death.

Πάλι η μουσική εκτρέπει τον αέρα
κι εγώ σκιάζομαι.

Να χορέψω τον φόβο;
Να μετριάσω την έπαρσή του;

Μετεωρίτες σκίζουν φυλλώματα,
πελώριοι κορμοί αστράφτουν
και σπάνε.

Θυμάμαι κάποτε σκεφτόμουν
πως θάμασταν ασφαλείς.

Once more music splits the air
and I'm afraid.

Shall I dance fear?
Shall I temper its vanity?

Comets slice through dense leaves,
enormous tree trunks light up and snap.

I recall when I thought
we would be safe.

Κάτι ανεβαίνει σαν καπνός
και αχνοβολώντας
μια κόκκινη αλεπού
διασχίζει το δάσος.
Η ουρά της πιάνει φωτιά.
Είμαι καλός σκοπευτής.

Something rises like smoke
and, loosing its smelly musk,
a red fox crosses the woods.
Its tail catches fire.
I'm a good shot.

Όνειρο είναι.
Αγαπώ τον κυνηγό,
το παιδί σ' εσένα.
Κοιμήσου ξανά.

Μια φορά κι ένα καιρό,
ήταν ένα αγόρι σ' εκείνο το πλοίο
κι έγραφε σ' ένα βιβλίο.
Ό, τι είχε ανάγκη να ιστορήσει
το έγραφε γρήγορα
με τη βιασύνη ενός επιζώντος.
Έξυνε τη σελίδα με τη γραφίδα
και τα πουλιά φτερούγιζαν
την αγωνία του.

It was only a dream.
I love the hunter,
the child in you.
Go back to sleep.

Once upon a time
there was a boy on a ship,
writing a book.
He wrote the story
he needed to tell quickly,
a survivor's haste.
The fountain pen scratched the page
as birds' wings beat out his agony.

Αθόρυβο, κολλημένο με στρείδια
το πλοίο φάντασμα παρασύρεται
στην ομίχλη, περνά την προβλήτα,
η άγκυρα σηκωμένη προ πολλού.

Το δωμάτιό της έχει λιγοστά έπιπλα·
προσπερνά το τρένο
και το τζάκι τρέμει.
Το μαύρο εκκρεμές
στο μαρμάρινο ράφι χτυπά.
Κοιτάζω τον καθρέφτη της
κι η λαίδη ξυπνά.

Noiselessly, the barnacled ghost ship
drifts in the mist,
passing the quay,
its anchor lifted long ago.

Her bedroom is sparsely furnished;
a train passes by, shaking the mantel.
On the marble shelf,
the black pendulum clock strikes.
I look in her mirror
and her ladyship wakes.

Όπως όλα ήμουν κι εγώ παροδική.
Δεμένος σε δέντρο ανυπόμονο
με κοίταξες.

Γρήγορο το γύρισμα του λαιμού σου.
Πολφώδης η σάρκα των καρπών.
Είναι το δάσος λησμονημένο
ή μάταιο ποίημα;

Πώς να μιλήσω για το δάσος;
Αυτό μόνο—
είχα επίγνωση της αναπνοής σου.

Like all else, I, too, was fleeting.
Tied to an impatient tree,
you gazed at me.

Your neck turned sharply.
The fruits' flesh decayed.
Is the forest forgotten
or is it a pointless poem?

How do I talk about the forest?
Only this—
I was alert to your breath.

Παχύ κέλυφος πάγου
στα δάχτυλά μου
και τα λιβάδια λάμπουν πυρίσπορα.
Πολική αντανάκλαση στον αέρα.
Ήσυχη νύχτα.

Ίσως να με αναζητήσεις.
Όμως εγώ μόλις σε δω
φιδίσιο φυτό θα γίνω, σου λέω
χαϊδεύοντας τον τροπικό
λαιμό του αλόγου μου.

Thick ice freezes on my fingers
and the meadows glow like embers.
A polar glistening in the air.
Peaceful night.

Perhaps you'll seek me.
Yet when I see you there,
I'll change into a snake plant, I tell you,
as I stroke the tropical
neck of my horse.

Ένα κομμάτι μου καθόταν
απέναντι απ' το πορτρέτο σου
και σε κοίταζε σαν να σου έγνεφε
ή να σε χαιρετούσε —

έγινες ήλιος σε σώμα ακέφαλο.

Εξόριστος στο φως,
υπάρχεις πέρα από το πρόσωπο.
Η πέτρα που δεν αγγίζεις
λάμπει κοντά στα δάχτυλα.

Είσαι και δεν είσαι
και είναι ήσυχα εδώ.

A part of me sat
facing your portrait
and she gazed at you, as if beckoning
or greeting you—

you changed to sun atop a headless body.

Exiled to light,
you exist beyond your face.
The stone you don't touch
shines near your fingers.

You are yet are not
and it is peaceful here.

Με βλέπεις να ισιώνω πτυχές,
να τυλίγω κορδέλες στις γάμπες
και περνάς στην αιωνιότητα
περιμένοντάς με να κλείσω τα μάτια.

Μαικήνα, κάποτε ήμουν
η γυναίκα σου.
Τι σήμαινε αυτό;
Ένα ερεθιστικό έκθεμα;
Μια δίνη μέσα στον χρόνο σου;

Δεν έγνεψες, δεν μίλησες.

Κι ακόμα δεν λες λέξη.

You watch me straightening my pleats
tying ribbons around my calves
and you pass into timelessness,
waiting for me to close my eyes.

I was once your wife, rich man.
What did it mean?
A titillating show?
A vortex in your years?

You did not beckon, did not speak.

You still don't say a word.

Κοίταζες προς το μέρος μου
από την άκρη στο βάθος.
Στους αρμούς του κορμού σου
αναδύονταν υδρόβια φύλλα
κι ανέπνεα απαλά.

Δεν επιθυμώ τίποτε απολύτως
από την περασμένη μας ζωή·
απλά περιφέρομαι
ανάμεσα στα δέντρα.

Το ποτάμι κυλούσε διάφανο.
Με ρώτησες, Τι σε φοβίζει ακριβώς;
Μπήκα στο δάσος με καλπασμό.

From the edge of distance, you eyed
where I was. Your torso's limbs sprouted
watery leaves and I breathed deeply.

I want absolutely nothing
from our past life;
I amble simply among the trees.

The river flowed translucent.
You asked, What exactly scares you?
I galloped far into the forest.

ACKNOWLEDGMENTS

Grateful acknowledgement is made to the journals in which these poems appeared:

American Poetry Review "I am the boy in a sailor suit," "Time was distilled," "I don't need black," "Raw refusal blows between us," "the scene needs nymphs," "You can tell sundry stories," "Black boots, cotton batiste camisoles," "Your eyes scanned me," "You touched me and I began to grow," "Petals sprinkle everywhere."

Persimmon Tree—an Online Journal of the Arts by Women Over Sixty: "I wear sunglasses with owl frames," "Once more music splits the air."

BIOGRAPHICAL NOTES

Photo credit: Nikos Pavlou

Liana Sakelliou is one of Greece's foremost literary figures, a poet, translator, critic, and editor. She is the author of twenty books, most recently: *Alchemy of Cells in a Painting Atelier,* selected poems in a bilingual edition (Linea, Bucharest, 2021), *Sequentiae,* a poetry collection (Gutenberg, Athens, 2021), *Where the Wind Blows Softly,* a poetry collection (Typothito, Athens, 2017), *Creative Reading, Writing, and Living: volume 1, The Novel,* co-authored with William Schultz (Gutenberg, 2013), *Prends-moi comme une photo,* a poetry collection (L' Harmattan, Paris, 2012), and the original Modern Greek version of *Portrait before Dark* (Typothito, 2010). She is the translator into Modern Greek of two of our most important American poets. In *Emily Dickinson: Because I could not bear to live aloud* (Gutenberg, 2013), she authored the critical introduction, co-translated 60 of Emily Dickinson's poems and edited the Greek translation of 165 letters. She co-translated and wrote the critical introduction to H.D.'s *Trilogy* (Gutenberg, 1999). She published a monograph on *Denise Levertov's Poetry of Revelation, 1988-1998: The Mosaic of Nature and Spirit* (Typothito, 2006) and on *Gary Snyder: The Poetics and Politics of Place* (Odysseas, Athens, 1998). Among her awards are two Fulbright Fellowships in the U.S., several fellowships from the British Council, the Marie Curie Intra-European Fellowship, the Stanley J. Seeger Visiting Research Fellowship at Princeton University, and residencies at West Dean College—University of Sussex, and at the Casa d' Escrita-Universidade de Coimbra—Portugal. She is Professor of English and Creative Writing at the National and Kapodistrian University of Athens and teaches International Poetry and Creative Writing at the Takis Sinopoulos Foundation. She served as President for the European Prize for Literature (EUPL) in 2017 and in 2018. Her poems have been widely anthologized and translated into ten languages.

Aliki Barnstone is a poet, translator, memoirist, critic, editor, and visual artist. Her first book of poems, *The Real Tin Flower* (Crowell-Collier, 1968), was published when she was 12 years old, with a foreword by Anne Sexton. In 2014, Carnegie-Mellon University Press published her book, *Madly in Love*, in the Carnegie Mellon Classic Contemporaries Series, which reissues the early work of America's important poets. Among her other six books of poetry are *Dear God Dear, Dr. Heartbreak: New and Selected Poems* (Sheep Meadow, 2009), *Bright Body* (White Pine, 2011), and *Dwelling* (Sheep Meadow, 2016). She translated *The Collected Poems of C.P. Cavafy* (W.W. Norton, 2006). Her translations have appeared in *The American Poetry Review, Crab Orchard Review, Virginia Quarterly Review, Triquarterly,* and elsewhere. The co-founder and former series editor of the Cliff Becker Book Award in Translation, she served twice as a translation judge for the National Endowment for the Arts. Liana Sakelliou's translation of Barnstone's *Eva's Voice* into Greek is forthcoming in a bilingual edition with Vakhikon Editions in Athens. She edited *A Book of Women Poets from Antiquity to Now* (Schocken,1980; 2nd edition, 1992) and the *Shambhala Anthology of Women's Spiritual Poetry* (Shambhala, 2002). Her criticism includes the introduction and readers' notes for H.D.'s Trilogy, co-editing *The Calvinist Roots of the Modern Era,* and her study, *Changing Rapture: The Development of Emily Dickinson's Poetry* (University Press of New England, 2007). She has been awarded a Senior Fulbright Fellowship in Greece, the Nevada Writers Hall of Fame Silver Pen Award, a Pennsylvania Council on the Arts Fellowship in Poetry, and residencies at the Anderson Center at Tower View and the Virginia Center for the Creative Arts. She is Professor of English at the University of Missouri and served as poet laureate of Missouri from 2016-2019.

Type Settings & Fonts:

GOUDY OLD STYLE – Goudy Old Style
PERPETUA TILTING MT
GARAMOND – Garamond

www.ingramcontent.com/pod-product-compliance
Lightning Source LLC
Chambersburg PA
CBHW020208090426
42734CB00008B/983